Granny's Colouring Book...
...and mine too!

Volume 4

I ♡ colouring with Granny

Janet McCormick

All rights reserved. No part of this publication may be reproduced in whole or in part, stored in any retrieval system, or transmitted in any form or by any means digitally, electronically, mechanically, by photocopying, by recording, or in any other manner, without prior permission from the author. Edited by C. McCormick. All designs copyright Janet McCormick. First published in 2020.

Colouring Tips

If you place a blank sheet of paper behind the page
you are about to colour, this will ensure
the following page is protected from any marks.

The last pages in the book are blank,
so you can take them out to use as
blotting sheets or colour test pages.

The designs are printed on one side only,
and there are wide margins,
so pages can be cut out for colouring,
or for display and framing.

Older kids can use a fine line black marker
to add more intricate patterns into the
simpler designs if they like.

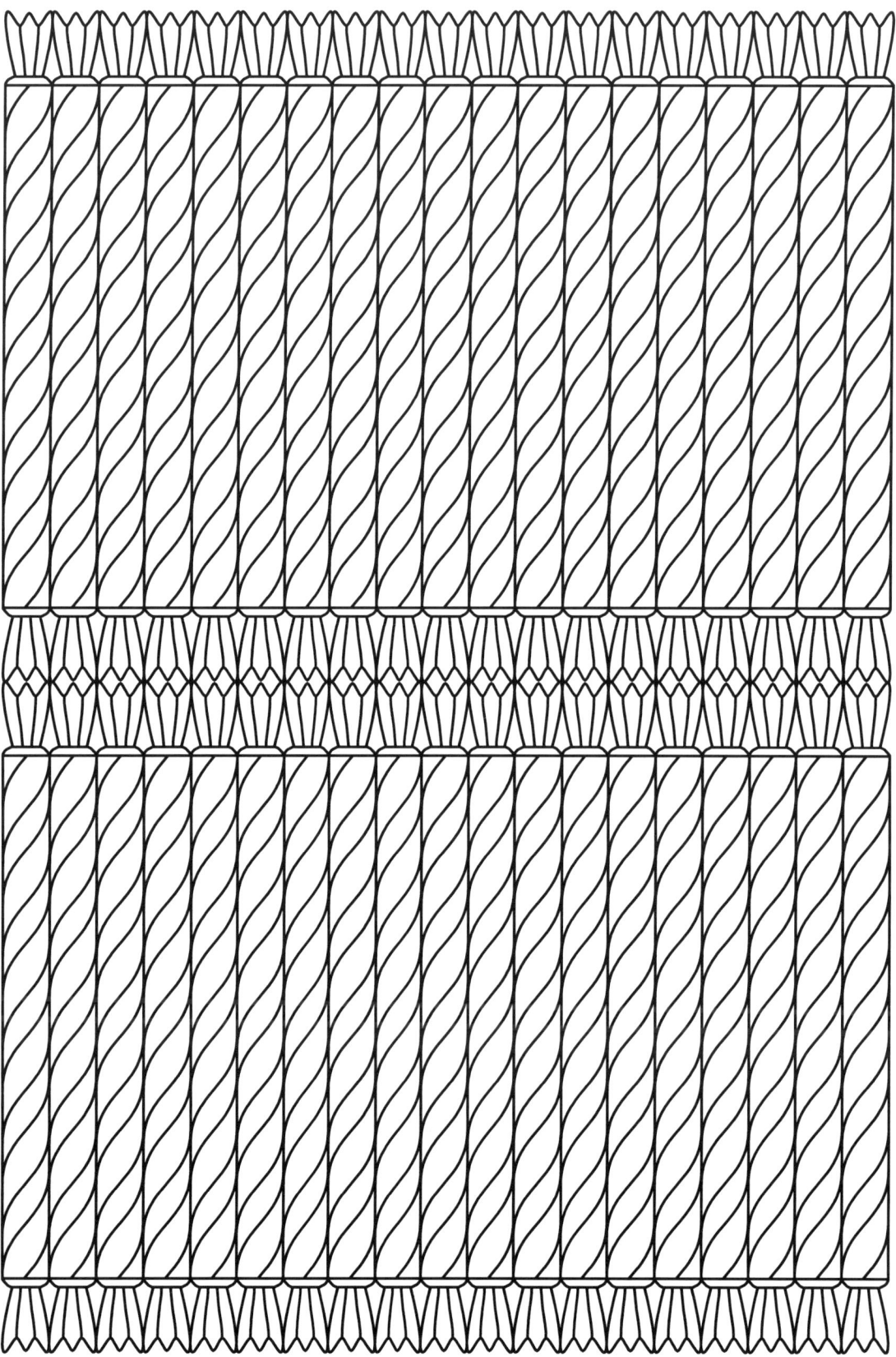

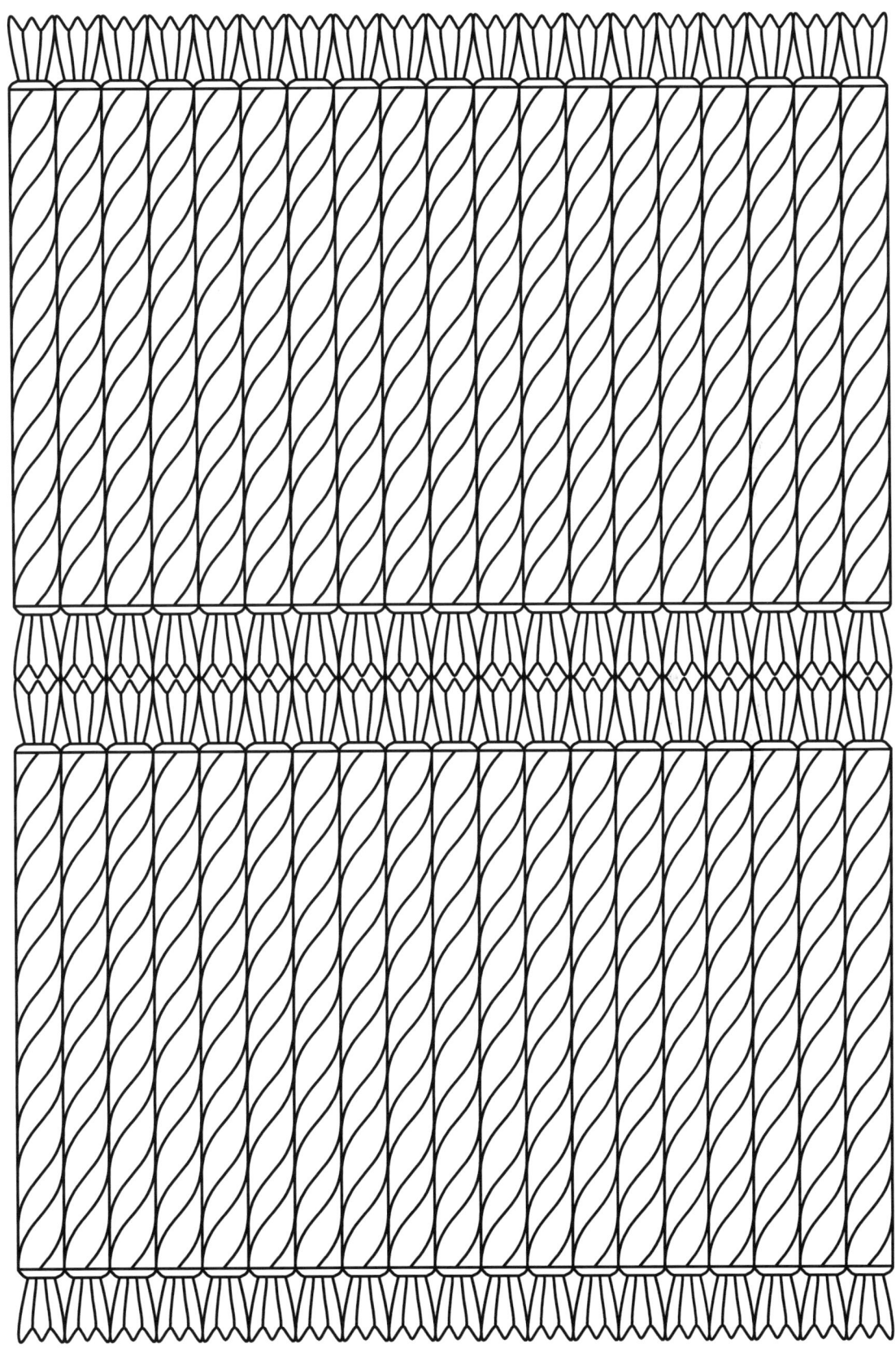

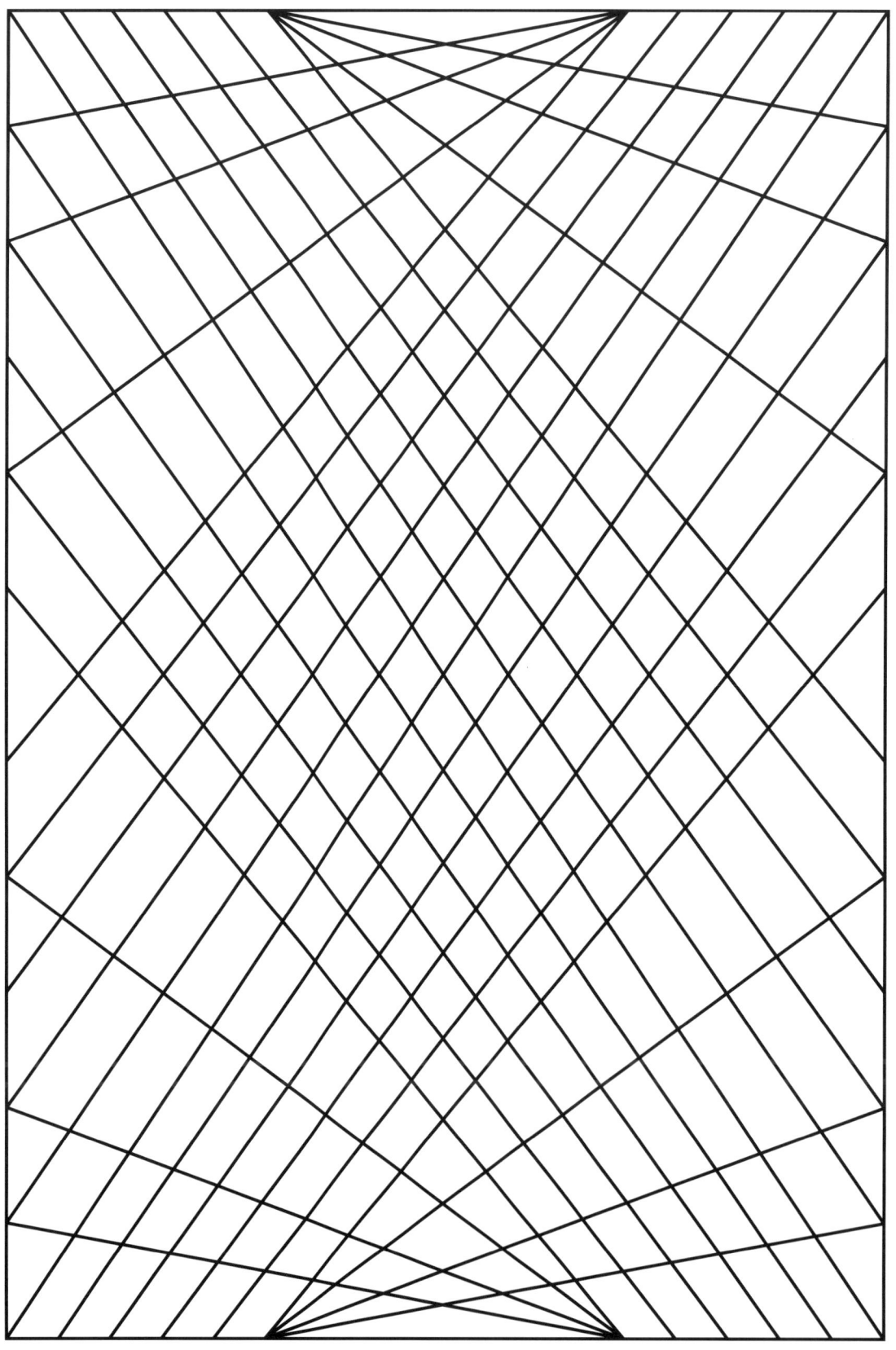

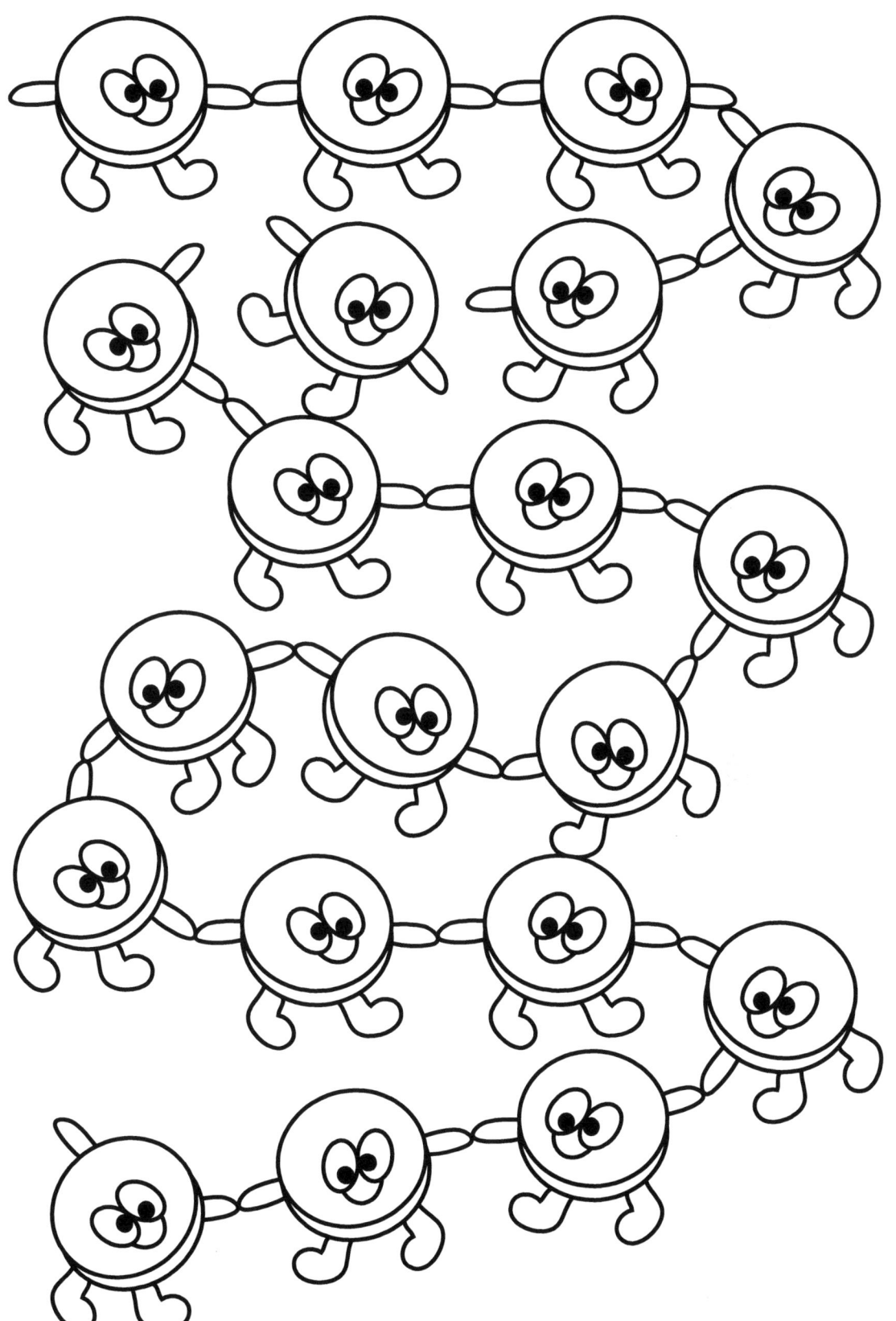

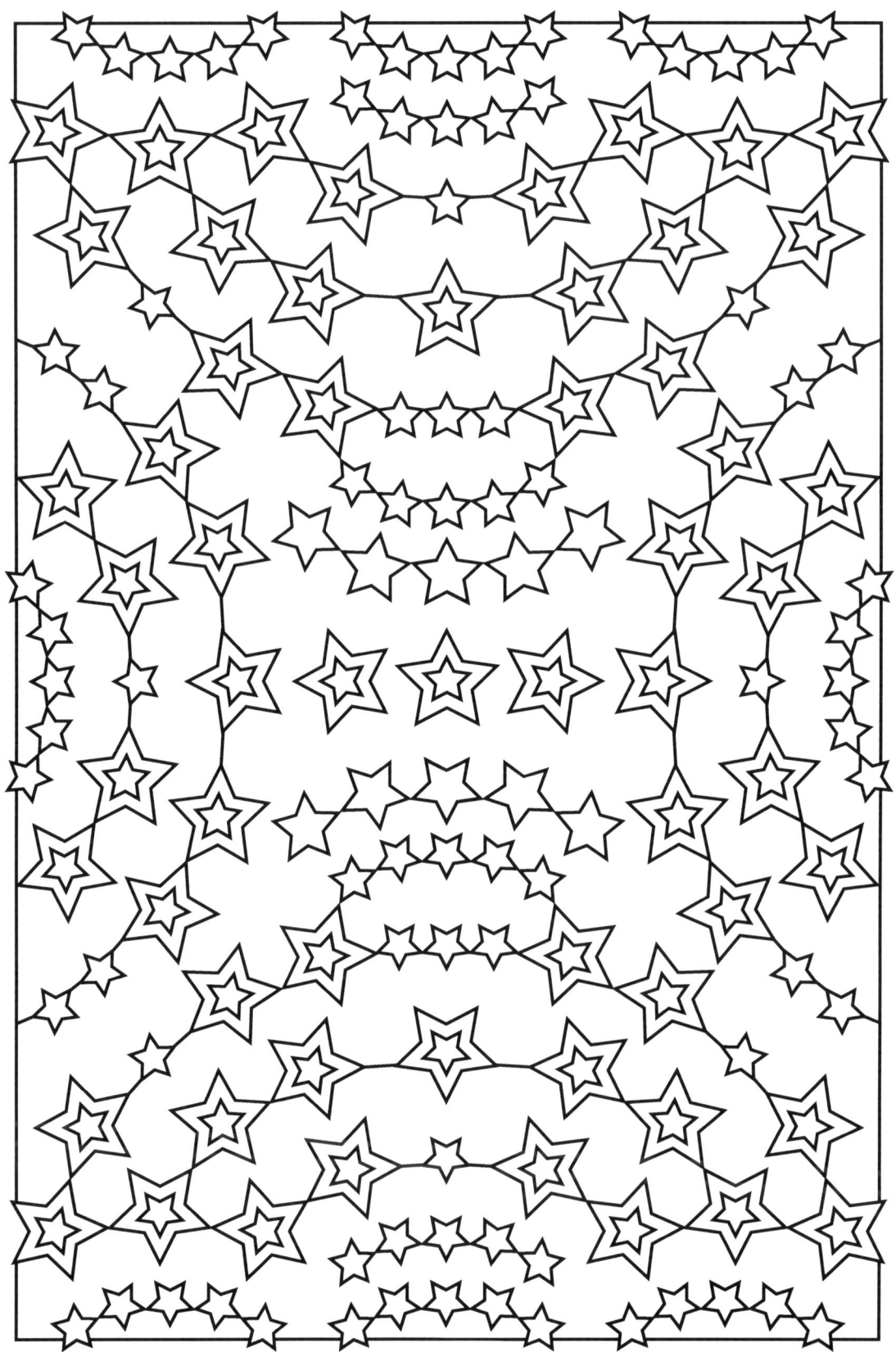

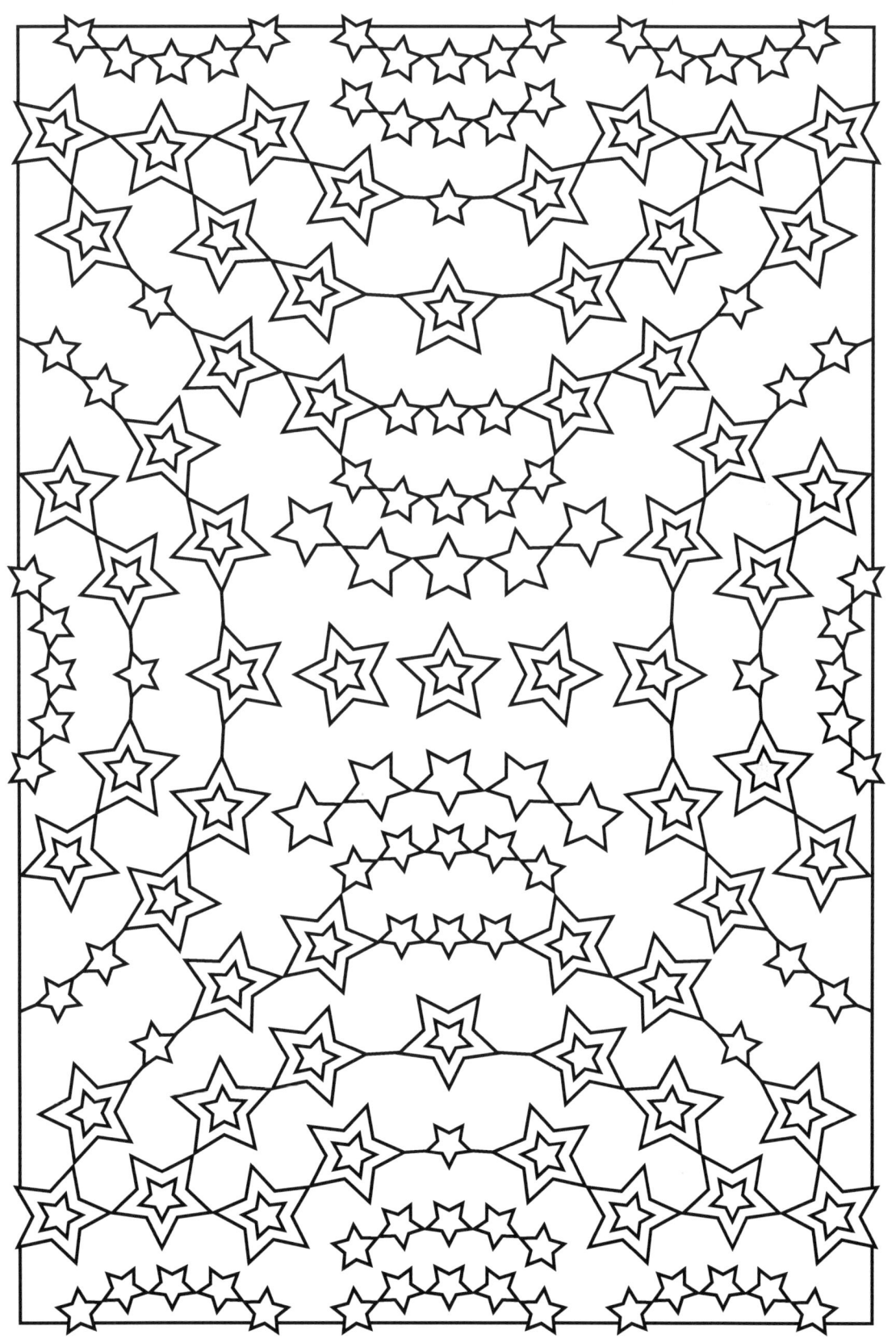

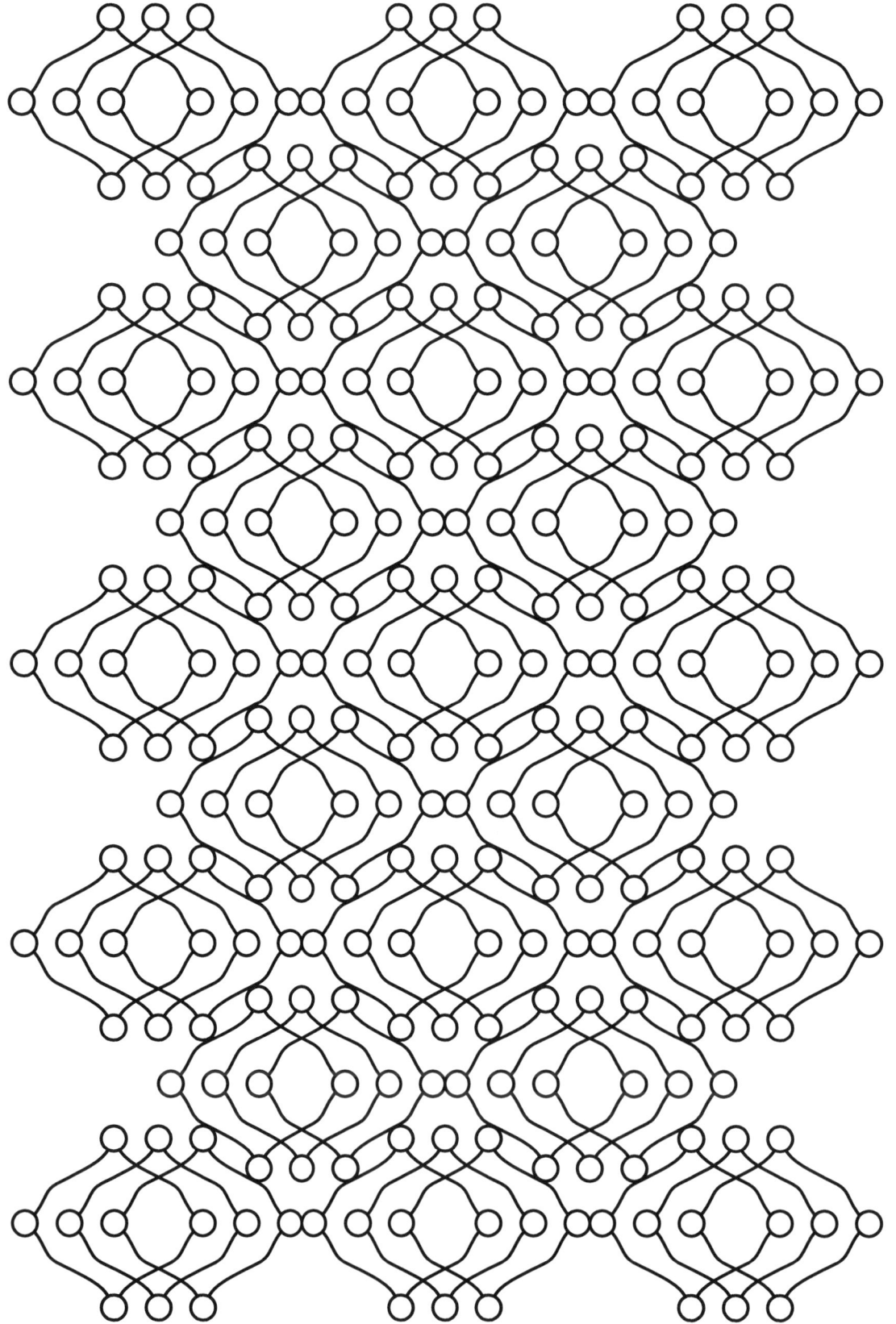

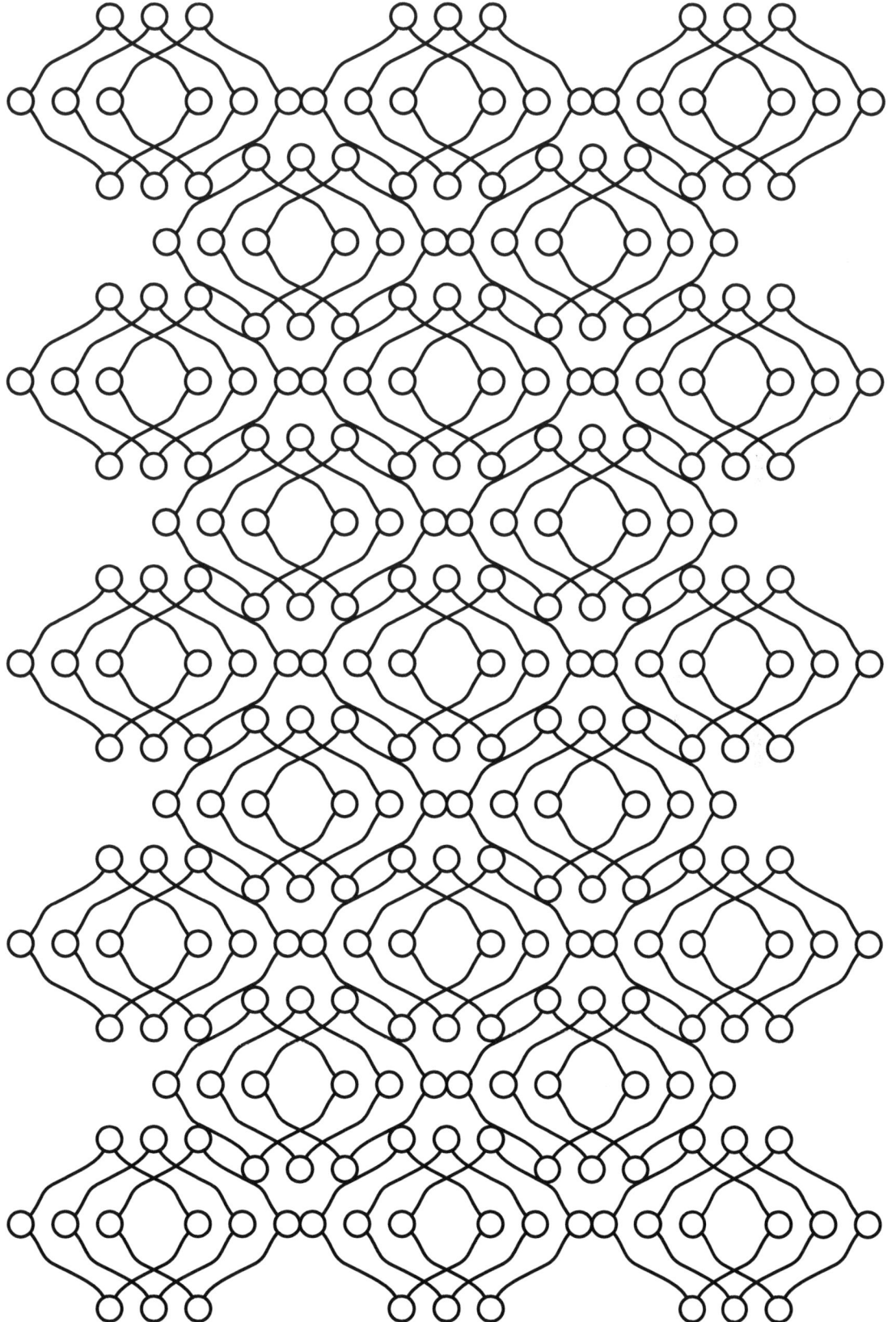

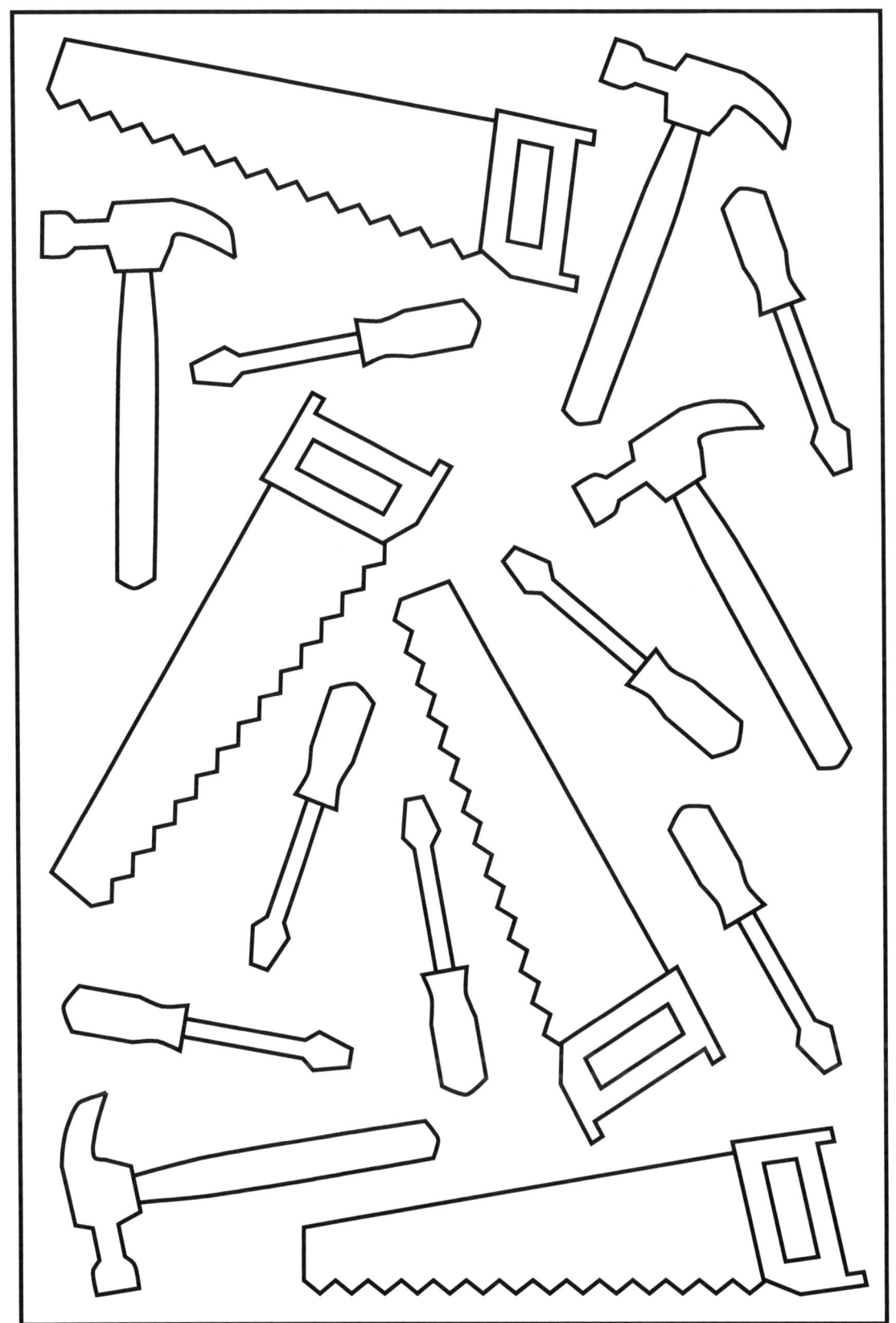

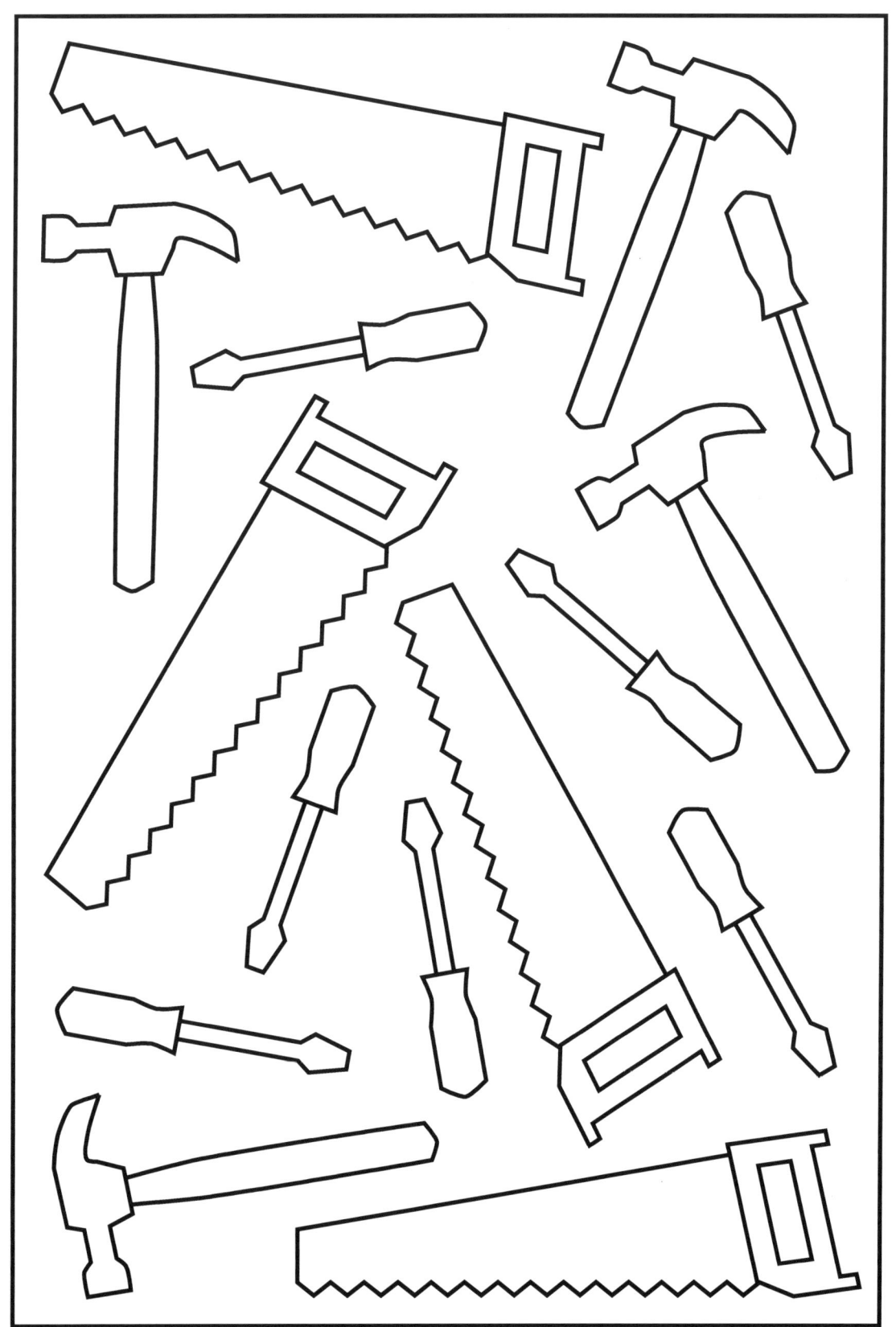

Blotting Sheets or Colour Test Pages

Blotting Sheets or Colour Test Pages

Printed in Great Britain
by Amazon